Dancing With Angels

Inspired Writings
By
Sandra J Yearman

Seraphim Publishing LLC

WE WILL BRING LIGHT TO ALL THE DARK PLACES

Registered trademark-Sandra J Yearman
Seraphim Publishing
438 Water St
Cambridge, WI 53523

Copyright © 2011 Sandra J Yearman
Produced in the United States of America
Author : Sandra J Yearman
Editor: Sandra J Yearman
Cover Design by Sandra J Yearman
Layout and design by Sandra J Yearman

All rights reserved. No part of this book may be reproduced, stored in or introduced into a retrieval system, or transmitted, in any form or by any means, electronic or mechanical, including photocopying or recording or otherwise copied for public or private use—other than for "fair use" as brief quotations embodied in articles and reviews-without written permission from the author.

Library of Congress Control Number: 2011913178

ISBN: 978-0-9841506-8-7

First Edition

On This Journey
Tests And Trials We Must Face
I Pray To God Upon My Knees
These Tests I Handle With Courage
And Grace
Amen
Amen
Amen

Contents

Dedication

To Dance Among Angels..................................7
Surrender...9
A Wedding Song......................................10
With His Breath......................................12
Thinking Of You......................................14
I Am My Brother's Keeper.......................15
God's Face...17
Angels Of Mercy.....................................19
Your Presence On This Earth...................20
God What Can I Do................................21
My Friend..23
A Song Of Promise.................................25

Seeking Light In The Darkness

In The Darkness Of My Anguish....................28
Reach Out Your Hand...............................30
Cries Into The Darkness............................31
Cancer..33
Love Has No Boundaries..........................35
Look For God Between The Words.............37

Contents

He Carried Me 39
The Sickness Of A Child 41
My Fears To Release 42
A Grateful Nation Weeps 44
He Took Me By My Hand 46
Who Saves The Warrior 48
Death Was Upon Her 50

Coming Home

The Spirit Descended On Him 53
God Is In The Silence 55
Angels Walked This Way 57
He Touched And Healed 59
Angels of Charity 61
Gratitude 63
I Will Be The Candle 65
The Gift I Was Given 67
Angels Dance 70

Dedication

To Dance Among Angels

To dance among Angels
To soar through the stars
To question eternity
To discover who we are

To follow the Voice inside
To listen to God Speak
To feel His Presence
His message to seek

Miracles among us
For our eyes to see
Clarity of sight
Connecting with Thee

Whispers in the silence
Love in the heart
Call out to the Father
Never be apart

Mysteries through the ages
Life with its tests
Know that God Loves you
Know you are blessed

When the illusions
No longer enhance
Call to the Heavens
And with Angels dance

Amen Amen Amen

Surrender

A word so very simple
In its meaning
Yet with its Truth
Can heal the human being

Believe that God will carry
Believe that God will heal
Surrender your heart to Him
On bended knees to kneel

He will carry you from the darkness
The broken and the worn
No disease can conquer Him
He will deliver you through the storm

Amen Amen Amen

A Wedding Song

Take my hand forever
Souls entwine as one
Love no more with boundaries
To you this song is sung

The circle is complete
My dreams have now come true
The half that I was living
Is whole with only you

Let creation sing with wonder
And stars dance in the sky
The poets through the ages
A love that will not die

Take my hand forever
Our lives we now complete
With oaths we swear to Heaven
With hearts that share one beat

Amen Amen Amen

With His Breath

He saved us from the darkness
He showed us how to conquer death
He blessed us with His Presence
He blessed us with His Breath

He opened up the Heavens
And let us hear God's Song
He saved us from our sins
He showed us how to correct
our wrongs

He showed us with His actions
He Graced us with His words
He sang the Songs of Heaven
Never before in this world heard

His Presence has never left us
With Him we are never alone
He promised He would carry
He showed us the Way back Home

Jesus is in the Silence
God is in the Song
The Spirit will ignite us
Their Love will make us strong

Amen Amen Amen

Thinking Of You

Angels whisper in the wind
Your name with thoughts of Love
As Heaven watches over
Blessings from Above

I heard the Song they whispered
I heard it in the wind
I send you love and blessings
Again and again

Know that we are with you
Alone you will never be
Angels sing you songs of Love
Their chants to set you free

Amen Amen Amen

I Am My Brother's Keeper

God help me not to be so
self absorbed
That I cannot see what is before
my eyes
That I am not aware
That I cannot hear the cries

God help me to remember
That my life here is shared
That I am my brother's keeper
That I cannot forget to care

God help me to remember
That creation is a gift
That all life is precious
That perception can shift

God help me to remember
That I am a child of Your Hand
That my spirit sores in Heaven
And is not limited to this world
of man

Amen Amen Amen

God's Face

Desperately they search for signs
And miracles to behold
They long to seek Your Face
To return back to the fold

They try to find Your Image
In all things man-made
But to seek the Face of God
Above this world to raise

God is with us always
He speaks to us each day
But we are afraid to listen
For fear of what others might say

God's Image is everywhere
In nature as we see
In Love for one another
In the Faith we have in Thee

Amen Amen Amen

Angels Of Mercy

For the mercy you give freely
For the kindness you spread with love
For the sorrow you dissipate
Know that Heaven watches from above

It takes a special being
To walk where others will not go
To care for people at their worse
Their destinies to know

God Bless you for your riches
The gifts you freely share
May God help you through the
difficult times
May you know that others care

Amen Amen Amen

Your Presence On This Earth

Moments filled with memories
Gifts from above
A life filled with riches
Blessings sent with Love

Think of the wonder
The creation of your birth
The lives that you have touched
Your presence on this earth

The Angels sing with Glory
At the gifts that God does create
Your life has blessed so many
The Hand of God elate

Amen Amen Amen

God What Can I Do

God every day we ask of You
Every day someone prays
For comforts and for healing
Some to seek the Holy Way

But how many of us offer
How many of us say
'God what would You like'
'Me to do this day'

The purpose that we have here
The reasons for our lives
Are hidden from most of us
As we are caught up in daily strife

But if we would ask You
If we would pray
Ask for Your guidance
As to be shown a Better Way

Perhaps the mysteries would
be answered
And we would clearly see
There is more to our lives here
If we would only ask Thee

Amen Amen Amen

My Friend

My friend so long, forever
The path we chose to take
The friendship that we shared
Only Heaven could create

This journey can be daunting
With its mysteries and its trials
True friendship has no boundaries
The risks we took worthwhile

Although separate pieces
Whole we were again
Creating new adventures
A life we would begin

Time, they say is fleeting
Man cannot control
The flow of life and death
Only Heaven really knows

Memories can be cherished
Or forgotten with the past
But true Love is eternal
Forever more to last

Amen Amen Amen

A Song Of Promise

Sing a song of promise
Sing a song of praise
To give thanks to God
For my blessings all my days

The darkness closed around me
His Voice I heard through the din
I called out for His Hand
He cradled me within

He healed the disease within me
He took away my fright
He blessed and consoled me
He saved me from the night

We sang a song together
He took away my pain
Together we will walk
Heaven to attain

Amen Amen Amen

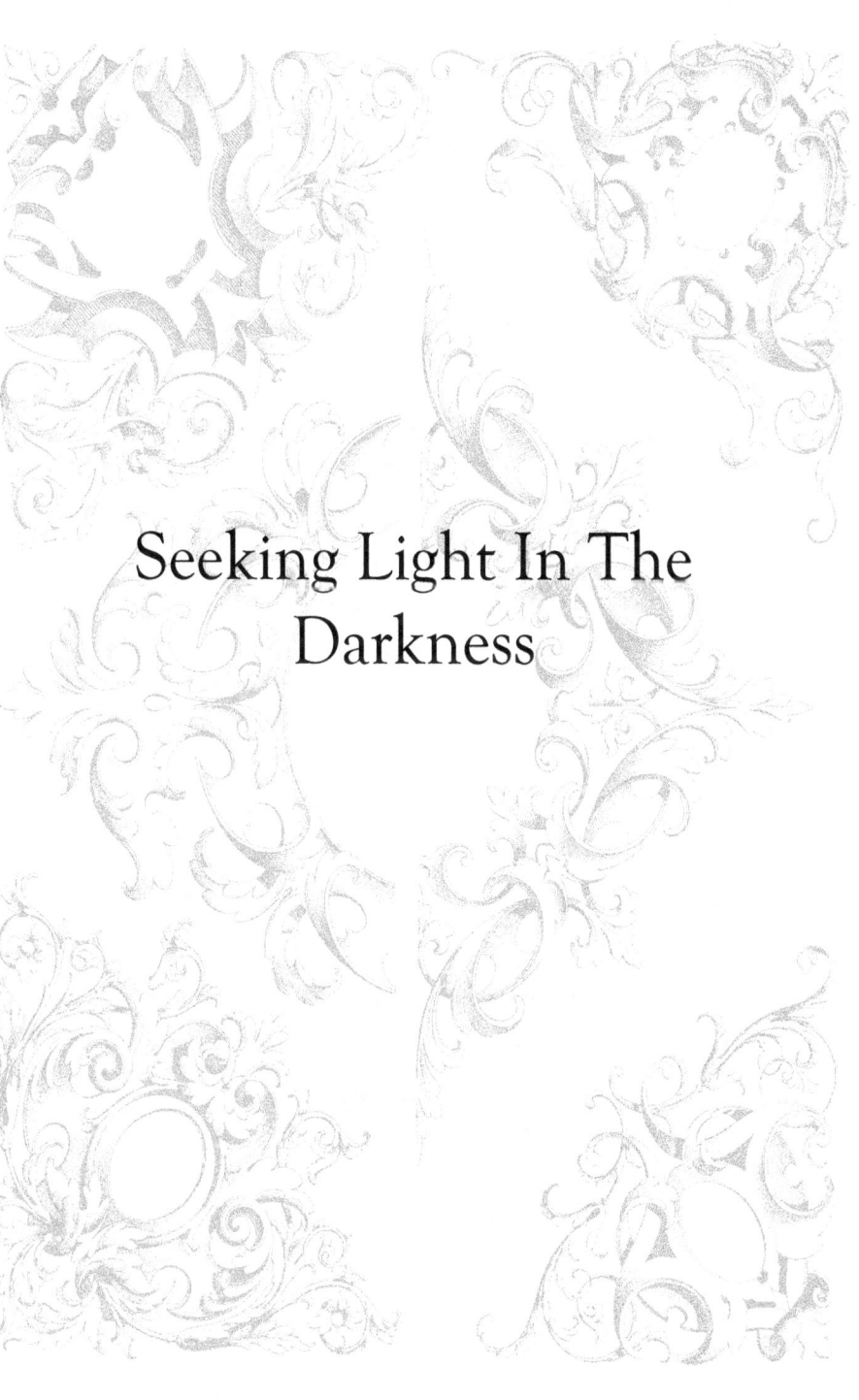

Seeking Light In The Darkness

In The Darkness Of My Anguish

The screams that I was hearing
Was a voice I recognized
I was screaming to the Heavens
I was crying to the skies

In the darkness of my anguish
In the pain I felt here
I was blinded to the Light
I felt the demons near

As my light extinguished
As I lost the fight
I cried out to the Heavens
To save me from the night

God showed me Mercy
And on that Christmas morn
He sent a friend to heal me
From a world consumed in scorn

The Angel He sent to me
A blessing and a gift
Changed my life forever
From darkness I was lift

Every Christmas morning
I am blessed with memories of
The greatest gift I received
My blessings from above

Amen Amen Amen

Reach Out Your Hand

God is always with you
At your bedside, Angels stand
When you feel alone and afraid
Simply reach out your hand

He will grasp on to it
Whether or not you can see
For He will never leave you
You are a child of Thee

Ask Him to carry
The fears that fill your heart
He will deliver you through the crisis
You will never be apart

Amen Amen Amen

Cries Into The Darkness

He cried out in the darkness
Consumed with pain and fear
Alone and abandoned
No one for to draw near

His body was broken and crippled
From ignorance and abuse
Did not anyone hear him
His crying was of no use

Lonely in the darkness
He cried out to be loved
God and all the Angels
Blessed him from above

Short his life on earth was
But before the end
God Blessed him with an Angel
A loving home and friends

All the years of loneliness
Darkness and despair
At the very end
He was surrounded by those
who truly cared

Amen Amen Amen

Cancer

I know you feel uncomfortable
With my situation
Please do not act like a cheerleader
What I need is for you to listen

Who is really in denial
When changes I try to explain
You do not want to hear
For a while there will be fatigue
and pain

Please do not project your fears
onto me
I have my own ways to cope
My faith in God
Is my strength and my hope

On this journey
Tests and trials we must face
I pray to God upon my knees
This test I handle with courage
and Grace

Amen Amen Amen

Love Has No Boundaries

Loss of a mother
Only Heaven knows
The grace she brought
The love she sowed

No one can take
Her place in your heart
Love has no boundaries
You will never be a part

God sends us Angels
In many forms
Heaven watches over
And holds you as you mourn

Know that God will carry
And heal your broken heart
Love has no boundaries
You will never be a part

Amen Amen Amen

Look For God Between The Words

God made us in His Image
Why does man pretend
To change the Image of God
To justify the darkness inside of man

Man has altered history
To justify their darkest needs
To promote their agendas
To glorify their deeds

We should never stop seeking
The Truth that God has sent
Sometimes man makes it difficult
To understand the Words that
God has meant

Ask that He will help you
Ask to be shown the Way
Listen for His Voice in the darkness
Speak to Him and pray

Ask Him to help you
To know and to understand
Ask Him to help you
Rise above the plight of man

Ask and He will answer
But be open to His Song
Ask to recognize the miracles
Know that God is never wrong

Amen Amen Amen

He Carried Me

I know that God is with me
I am not frightened in this place
I sing the song of Heaven
I have been blessed by Holy Grace

I asked that He would carry
And Blessings I did receive
When I prayed unto the Heavens
With my heart I do believe

I had to take a journey
Some say a walk through hell
But, God He walked it with me
And I live this day to tell

The journey, although arduous
Was lessened by His Might
For when I was too weak
He carried me through the night

Amen Amen Amen

The Sickness Of A Child

God will send an Angel
To hover over your bed
To put His arms around you
To kiss you on your head

Ask God to help you
When you are afraid and weak
And He will send you Angels
Listen for them to speak

God will never leave you
Even when the way seems long
When you are scared
Sing to God a Song

Amen Amen Amen

My Fears To Release

I stared into the darkness
My body racked with pain
Afraid to hear the doctor's words
The cancer had returned again

As my eyes did focus
I thought it was a dream
A figure floated above me
I did not speak, I did not scream

I heard the nurses talking
But they did not seem to see
The figure that I saw
The figure that appeared to me

When I realized it was an Angel
My fears, they were released
My worries no longer controlled me
My soul was filled with peace

I knew it was a sign from God
An answer to a prayer
I had asked that He would carry
My burdens He would share

I knew that I was not alone
Nor would I ever be
I called out to the Heavens
I felt the Presence of Thee

Amen Amen Amen

A Grateful Nation Weeps

The Angels sing with Glory
As a grateful nation weeps
Another warrior carried Home
All Holiness to keep

Some surpass the boundaries
This human world creates
Some soar above
The darkness and the hate

The warriors of this world
Who with honor shown
The duty and the bravery
Our nation's protectors known

God bless the families
The comrades and the free
God bless the warriors
Who on bended knees

Ask for a better world
Fight for a Better Way
Pay the ultimate price
That others may live a brighter day

Amen Amen Amen

He Took Me By My Hand

The shadow loomed before me
The darkness and the cold
I feared the journey I would take
My life might be the toll

I walked into the valley
I saw so many fall
I heard their cries in the night
I tried but could not call

I prayed unto the Heavens
To help me in my plight
To save me from the shadow
To guide me in the night

And God in all His Mercy
Heard the prayers I said
He took me by my hand
And through the valley I was led

As long as I was with Him
My fears ceased to be
The darkness could not conquer
The shadow no longer scared me

We are still walking
The valley we left behind
The night could not hold us
God's Grace I did find

Amen Amen Amen

Who Saves The Warrior

He sat in his shelter
Listening to the voices of the dead
The screams and the terror
Inhabited his head

War after war
Pieces remain
In the spirit and the body
In the horror and the pain

Warriors among us
Wounds that will not heal
The demons they fought
The demons still real

Discarded and homeless
No shelter, no bread
Who saves the warrior
When his spirit is dead

God bless Your children
Help them to heal
Conquer their demons
Let them know You are Real

Amen Amen Amen

Death Was Upon Her

Her body was frail beyond belief
Her eyes wide from hunger
Cradled in her mother's arms
Death was upon her

God's children are everywhere
Every creed and every color
Do we turn our eyes
And allow death to be upon her

They walked to flee the armies
That butchered and that maimed
So many died along the way
And yet nobody came

Sold into slavery
So parents could feed the others
Demons bought them in the night
They cried for their mothers

God's children are everywhere
Every creed and every color
Do we turn our eyes
And allow death to be upon her

God save your children
The ones who suffer
And the ones who watch

Amen Amen Amen

Coming Home

The Spirit Descended On Him

The Spirit descended on Him
The Son that God sent
The very sign from Heaven
God's Grace as it was meant

Glory Alleluia
Did the Angels sing
Glory Alleluia
The Spirit forth to bring

Miracle of Miracles
A Holy sign from above
That God would Bless and care for
This holy life with love

Now let us surrender
And to the Father pray
God Bless our loved one
On this Holy day

Amen Amen Amen

God Is In The Silence

When we think God does not hear us
When we think we are alone
When we think that He has left us
His Love to us is shown

God will never leave you
He is in the silence and the song
Ask that He will hold you
In His hands our hearts belong

Our eyes can be clouded
By the darkness and our fear
Just because we cannot see Him
Does not mean that God is not near

Stretch your hand to hold His
Raise your voice in prayer
Know that He hears you
And His Presence is always there

God will never leave you
He is in the silence and the song
Ask that He will hold you
In His hands our hearts belong

The boundaries of this world
Limit what we see
Put your faith in His Will
Ask to walk with Thee

Amen Amen Amen

Angels Walked This Way

Sometimes upon this journey
The shadows they play tricks
We think that God is punishing us
Because we are injured, we are sick

How does life have meaning
Without the challenges and the tests
Pray to God to conquer
The darkness and the death

We get so lost in darkness
We fear that God will let us go
Yet He will walk there with us
If you ask His Presence to know

God does not forget us
Or in the darkness leave
The choices are ours to make
To sink or to believe

When you are crying in the darkness
And the dawn brings a better day
Know that God has blessed you
And Angels have walked this Way

Amen Amen Amen

He Touched And Healed

He touched and healed
God's children here
The Son of Heaven
Brought God near

There is no illness
That can withstand
The touch of God's
Holy hands

Have faith in Him
Call out His name
Ask Him to carry
Ask Him to reclaim

Your heart and soul
That He created
A covenant made
And long awaited

Amen Amen Amen

Angels of Charity

Angels walk among us
Their Charity is shown
In the kindness of the words
In the Love and Hope that is known

God sends us miracles
And gifts we do not always see
Some give us comfort
Others set us free

Love is in the kindness
The gentleness of a touch
To those sick with despair
Mean ever so much

Angels walk among us
Their presence to heal
The gifts that God sends us
His Love that is real

Even in our darkest days
Know we are not alone
Ever is the candle
The flame showing the
way back Home

Amen Amen Amen

Gratitude

I know that God walked with me
I know He held my hand
As the doctors treated me
To eradicate a scourge of man

I know I felt His Presence
During the tests and surgeries
Throughout the chemotherapy
and radiation
I know He was with me

I heard His Voice speak softly
As He dissolved my fears
I felt the presence of His Hand
As it wiped away my tears

As I walked this journey
As dark as it could be
I realized the many miracles
I found surrounded me

I was never alone in the darkness
There was always a Light
Since I had asked God
To walk with me in the night

Now the treatments have ended
And I am well again
I never could have made this journey
If I would not have asked God in

Thank You God

Amen Amen Amen

I Will Be The Candle

I am not going to leave you here
In the darkness of the night
I will stay with you always
And deliver you from your fright

I will be the candle
That shows you Holy Light
I will be the Angel
That protects you from the night

I will be your anchor
I will be your net
I will be your cord
For I AM Heaven sent

I AM the Answer
I AM the Lamb
I AM your Father
I AM Who I AM

Amen Amen Amen

The Gift I Was Given

Some said it was a death sentence
Others said a curse from Heaven
In truth, when they told me
I had cancer
I never realized the gift I had
been given

So much time I had wasted
On darkness and on stress
I never before realized
How my life was blessed

We take so much for granted
We fail at priorities
When they told me I had cancer
I got down on my knees

'God I know there is a reason'
'For every walk in life'
'I pray that You will carry me'
'Through the pain and through
the strife'

He never left me on my journey
He stayed with me through the tests
I learned to see with eyes anew
To see differently than the rest

I saw more beauty in the world
I was filled with charity
My heart was filled with gratitude
My soul with clarity

Although this journey is not over
I am doing well
I put my faith in God
And broke the chains of hell

I make more time for beauty
My life I now enhance
I take more time for music
I now ask God to dance

Amen Amen Amen

Angels Dance

Angels dance
To ancient Songs
The Love of God
That brings us Home

Songs of Glory
Songs of Grace
With the promises
To the human race

Angels dance
To the Song of Love
To a King who was sent
From God above

Angels dance
With Holy glee
Because God's Love
Will set man free

Amen Amen Amen

Thank You For The Journey
Without I would Not See
That Death Can Be Conquered
That Miracles Are Sent From Thee
Amen
Amen
Amen

www.ingramcontent.com/pod-product-compliance
Lightning Source LLC
Chambersburg PA
CBHW051714040426
42446CB00008B/882